Leather Working Book for Beginners

A Leather Crafting Starter Handbook of 15 Leather Craft Projects Plus Tips, Tools and Techniques to Get You Started

By

Luke Byrd

Copyright © 2021 – Luke Byrd

All rights reserved

No part of this publication may be reproduced, distributed, or transmitted in any form or by any means, including photocopying, recording, or other electronic or mechanical methods, without the prior written permission of the publisher, except in the case of brief quotations embodied in reviews and certain other non-commercial uses permitted by copyright law.

Disclaimer

This publication is designed to provide competent and reliable information regarding the subject matter covered. However, the views expressed in this publication are those of the author alone, and should not be taken as expert instruction or professional advice. The reader is responsible for his or her own actions.

The author hereby disclaims any responsibility or liability whatsoever that is incurred from the use or application of the contents of this publication by the purchaser or reader. The purchaser or reader is hereby responsible for his or her own actions.

Table of Contents

Introduction 7

Chapter 1 9

Essentials of Leather Crafting 9

    What is Leather Crafting? 9

    History of Leather Crafting 10

    Reasons for Leather Crafting 12

Chapter 2 14

Leather Crafting Techniques 14

    Leather Selection and Storage 14

    Cutting Leather 18

    Coloring Leather 19

    Skiving Leather 22

    Gluing Leather 23

    Burnishing Leather 23

    Saddle Stitching 29

Applying Finishes to Leather Strips 31

Cleaning and Conditioning Leather 34

Stamping 35

Carving 37

Chapter 3 39

Leather Crafting Tips and Tricks 39

Chapter 4 44

Getting Started with Leather Crafting 44

Leather Crafting Tools and Supplies 44

Leather Material 44
Working Surface 50
Sewing Thread 51
Pencils, Paper, and Cardboard 51
Straight-Edged Ruler or Steel Square 52
Scratch Awl 52
Knife and Leather Shears 52
Rubber Cement and White Glue 53
Latex Gloves 53
Strap Cutter 53
Tracing Film 53
Modeling Tools 54
Brushes or Wool Daubers 54

Water Container, Sponge, and Spray Bottles 54
Tooling Surface 55
Swivel Knife 55
Metal Stamping Tools... 55
Mallet 56
Edge Beveller... 56
Hole Punches 56
Setters... 57
Pear Shader.. 57
Veiner... 58
Seeder... 58
Setting Up Your Leather Crafting Workshop 58

Leather Crafting Safety Measures 60

Chapter 5 62

Leathercraft Project Ideas 62

Leather Cat Purse 62

Leather Tassel Sandals 72

Leather Earrings 75

Leather Valet Tray 77

Leather Flannel Snap Scarf 81

Leather Tablet Case 86

Leather Camera Strap.. 98

Leather Clutch Bags 104

Leather Mason Jar Sleeve 111

Leather Magazine Holder 116

Mini Leather Pouch 122

Yoga Mat Strap 125

Fold-Over Clutch 127

Mouse Pad 129

Leather Studded Bracelet 131

Chapter 6 134

Fixing Common Leathercraft Problems 134

Conclusion 145

Introduction

Leather is one of the oldest and most valuable materials in the world today, as it helped solved a lot of issues in the past, and even now. Its general-purpose setting was what made it sail through the realms of time, and you would agree with me that both men and women can rock with leather. You could make leather shoes, books, jewelry, gloves, and even garments! Before you wonder how ludicrous it would be to put on leather, take a minute to think about your leather coats and how warm they keep you in the cold weather. In fact, this leather was that the early men used to protect themselves from the coldness of the weather and protect the soles of their feet as they roamed the earth.

Leather can be obtained naturally from the skin and hides of animals, and most times, they are tanned to become actual leather. So, now, to craft this leather into beautiful and artistic projects, you would need to be guided to prevent errors and general wastage of material. That is why this book, **Leather Working Book for Beginners**, was written, with every necessary detail that will guide you into making those brilliant projects.

The good thing is that the details were penned down with so much carefulness that you'd almost feel like the book was some kind of physical teacher.

In this book are safety precautions, tips, techniques, and important project descriptions that will make your journey into the art of leather crafting a big bliss. You will learn how to mold, shape, embellish, lace, stitch, glue, sew, color, and finish leather strips in this outline, and that will lead you to the prime of what leather crafting actually is. You will also learn of other basic techniques like burnishing, stitching, sanding, and braiding. And you can be sure that all of these things will last you till forever and beyond. All you need do is just to exercise a lot of patience, and see how you can fuse your creativity into the work you do.

So, let's begin, crafters.

Chapter 1

Essentials of Leather Crafting

What is Leather Crafting?
Leather crafting is an art that deals with the cutting, stamping, folding, and decoration of leather. The art makes maximum use of scrap pieces of leather that are sourced from torn leather jackets, discarded leather purses, worn billfolds, kid's gloves, etc. And after several useful techniques, you end up getting even more beautiful finished leather products. Leather is a natural material that mostly comes from the bodies of animals like buffaloes, goats, pigs, and some other rare animals like alligators and kangaroos. However, getting this leather means that some animals have to be killed, cowhides have been processed into so many forms that mimic the quality of the skins of other animals. You would be using cowhide for the majority of the leather crafting projects. Examples of the projects you can make with leather include belts, footwear, horse gear, armor, sheaths, drums, and pouches. The art also employs techniques like hand-stitching, lacing, and braiding in

the construction of leatherwork projects. The other techniques include the actualization of shaping techniques, coloring techniques—dyeing and painting—carving, stamping, molding, shaping, etching, perforation of holes, and even pyrography.

History of Leather Crafting

The use of leather dates back to more than five hundred thousand years ago, and the story guarding its advent was tied to the absence of technology in the stone age. The early men majorly fed on animals, and one issue was that they didn't have any means of preserving the bodies of their kills. Worms would have their share of the meat the longer it stayed on the ground, and that was one big issue for them. So, because the meat got unfit for consumption rather quickly, they had to kill a lot of animals day after day. And as expected, it led to a lot of meat getting wasted.

So, after a lot of thinking, the early men decided to save some parts of the animals that they killed from joining the heaps of wasted meat. And it was at that time that the value of the animal skins was discovered. It was tough, impermeable to water, and after being processed by fire, it became even more valuable. It was a better covering for them than the leaves of plants, as its thickness shielded them from the brutality of the cold. It was also very effective in protecting the soles of their feet while they walked about the earth. The most important of its function was that it was used as a means of shelter.

As time passed by, human beings began to see these animal skins, i.e., leather, in a new light. So, instead of just utilizing them for the production of clothes and shoes, better ideas came, and they were used for making soldier's shields and jewelry. Leather became more fashionable, and was used to make sandals, handbags, belts, saddles, and even sleeping tents! The use of leather boomed into something big and fiery when its quality and the general outlook was improved by synthetic procedures like tanning, painting, dyeing, carving, shaping, stamping, and molding. These new ideas made the leather strips produce even more beautiful aprons and hats.

When machines got involved in the production of leather, the idea of tanning the strips differently came up, and Chromium was used for the process. Before the idea of Chromium tanning came into existence, what was used was the vegetable tanning method, and the difference lay in the fact that the former produced leather products that were much softer and thinner. Now, in the present world, you could easily find leather in several colors, and structures, with it playing out several uses.

Reasons for Leather Crafting

You might wonder why the art of leather crafting has stolen the hearts of many people today. Here, you will find out a couple of reasons behind it.

1. Leather can be used to produce a wide range of objects, and they include bags, shoes, gloves, coats, book covers, and so many other beautiful things. It's the general purpose of leather today that makes a lot of people love it. It having a general-purpose means that it attends to the needs of both women and men, and that is another big plus. So, when talking about projects like jewelry for women, you could work with leather. And for men, you could make journals, wallets, belts, etc.
2. Leather is one of the most durable crafting materials anyone could work with, and so, no

matter the number of years you use it, it still retains its quality, texture, strength, and smell!
3. With leather, you can get to work on your creative abilities. There are a thousand and one things leather can be used for that haven't even been discovered yet, and its versatility ensures this fact. So, once you understand the major techniques, you can try making the various things you have stored up in your head.
4. Leather can be used as means of preserving legacies and traditions. Leather is one material that has survived the test of time, and even when you visit most of the museums today, you would see several leather works that were crafted years ago. In some other cities, the kings have several leather embodiments that were passed down to them from their forefathers.
5. The end result of leather crafting is usually a big icing on the cake, as you come out with extremely beautiful and ornate finished projects.

Chapter 2

Leather Crafting Techniques

When making crafts with leather, there are several things that you should take note of to aid the execution of projects. In this section, we would discuss the various techniques involved in making leather crafting projects.

Leather Selection and Storage

This is one factor that determines the success and the overall quality of your finished leather works. And it is so sad that even with the seeming simplicity of this stage, a lot of people have gone wrong with it. To avoid issues, you must take note of all the points that will be raised here.

- When you want to get a leather strip for your project, you price it per square foot, regardless of whatever part—side, shoulder—that you plan on using. If you aren't too sure about what part of the leather to work with for your projects, you could start first by getting a double shoulder hide.

- You should also consider what you will be using the leather strips for. The purpose determines the size of leather you will be getting. For example, to make a long belt, you will need a strip of leather that is long enough to be cut out in one piece.
- When getting your leather, examine it for defects. Most of the full-grained leather strips have several scars that could mar the beauty of your finished projects, and you wouldn't want that. However, some projects may require these natural defects, so you could decide to go for those types, while creatively working them out so that they still look attractive.
- Leather is best stored by keeping the strips loosely folded with the grainy side inwards. You should also see that you store the leather in a cool and dry place.
- As a beginner, you should get used to the following classes of leather and their overall thickness.
    - For key holders, you will need a leather whose thickness ranges from 4 to 5 oz.
    - For cardholders, the thickness of the leather should range from 4 to 5 oz.

- For belts, the thickness should range from 7 to 10 oz.
- For pet leashes, the thickness should range from 7 to 8 oz.
- For cellphone leashes, the thickness should range from 4 to 5 oz.
- For wallets, the thickness should range from 4 to 5 oz.

- The thickness of leather strips is measured in ounces, and one ounce is equal to 1/64-inch thick leather. The density of leather varies throughout the span of the hide, so most times, it's usually described as having a thickness that ranges between six and seven ounces.
- There are different kinds of leather. There is the vegetable-tanned leather, and this is the one you should go for when making projects that require firm and hard leather. It is also the only kind of leather that you can easily work tools through. The other type of leather is the chrome tanned leather that was tanned with chemicals like chromium salts. You will need this kind of leather for projects that require soft and very flexible

leather. Note that chrome-tanned leather strips cannot be tooled!
- The buffalo leather is what you need for making shoes, boots, and other small leather goods. It is as coarse as pigskin, and it comes in inches as long as 40 square feet.
- Cowhide is very good for footwear, furniture, car upholstery, saddles, belts, and so on. It is also the commonest leather you will find in the market, and it is the best for making handbags. It is a durable, and tool-friendly material that can be as thick as 16 ounces. It can either exist as vegetable-tanned or chrome-tanned.
- The lightweight of deerskin makes it very suitable for gloves and garments. It has a length that runs through a range of seven to twelve inches.
- Goatskin is a tough and durable leather that is mostly finished in bright colors. This leather is what you will need for women's shoes and cowboy boots.
- Another thing we should consider under this section is the weight of the leather you need for your projects. For light bags, like purses that need

to be made with very durable leather, you can go for the 4-5-ounce leather. If the bag is to have compartments, you can work with the 4-5-ounce leather for light bags. Then, use the 3-4-ounce leather for the interior.

Cutting Leather

Cutting out strips of leather wrongly can be one of the most catastrophic things that could ever happen to you as a beginner. This craft requires that you strictly follow your outlined measurements to get your projects looking the same way you intended them to look. For this process, you will need different tools, all depending on the kind of projects you are working on. The cutting tools include rotary cutters, utility knives, round knives, and so on. As you work, you will go on to find what suits you best, but then, in the meantime, as a beginner, you can use a rotary cutter to cut through leather strips as thin as one or two oz. For thick leather strips, you can use utility knives.

The rotary knife is the tool you will need for cutting through the leather that is light enough for garments, and upholstery. It is also the best tool for making straight cuts. To cut with this knife, you can either push it through the leather or draw the tool through it. The only issue with this tool is that it cannot cut tight corners, and the blades also cannot be easily sharpened.

Utility knives, also known as box cutters, can be used for making intricate cuts and cutting through tight corners. These kinds of cuts are ones that the rotary cutters may not be able to handle. Utility knives are easy to work with, super comfortable, and most importantly, are equipped with blades that can be changed easily. Lastly, because utility knives can be used for most projects, you can go for it as a beginner, instead of buying other costlier and specific-purpose knives.

Also, when getting a leather cutting tool, ensure that you go for ones that have snap-off blades that have sharp cutting edges. A craft knife works well for light-weight leather. Leather shears on the other hand are good for light-weight leather too, but the downside to them is that they don't make cuts as accurate as the ones the other knives make.

Coloring Leather

You can make your leather projects more attractive to the eye by staining them with dyes. Well, some projects need not be stained if you need to maintain their natural colors. You can use several techniques to color your projects, and one of them is the background dyeing technique. It helps to add extra depth to your projects. Before you carry out this technique on your project, though, ensure that you practice first on some scrap piece of leather. Below are some terminologies associated with the coloring of a leather strip.

- **Background Dyeing:** For this procedure, you will need leather dyes, a quality brush, a good finish, scrap pieces of leather, and paper towels. Start by running the tip of your brush that has already been soaked into a pot of finish across the surface of a scrap piece of leather. This technique will ensure that the excess dye is squeezed out of the brush. Too much dye will only cause the surface of your project to bleed. To apply dyes, start from the middle of the area you want to color so that even if bleeding occurs, it will only extend to the other parts you want covered. Before you apply

any kind of leather finish, wait for the dye to completely dry out first.
- **Coloring of large areas:** For this technique, you will need leather dyes, aerosol sprays, protective paper, and finishes. You can start by spraying one side of your project. Once the spray comes out smoothly, you can then begin to move the mouth of the spray across the surface of the project smoothly in even lines. Ensure that you watch out for drips! Do not apply another coat of color unless the previous one has dried completely! When you are done applying all the layers, wait for the project to dry. Then, you can use a clean roll of cotton wool or a lint-free cloth to get rid of the excess dye. Lastly, apply any finish of your choice to the project.
- **Leather stains:** Here, use a slightly moist sponge to apply the stains to the surface of your project. Apply it in circles until the color is even and all the cuts are filled. Leave the project to dry for some time. Next, use a moist sponge to get rid of the excess stain until you get the look you want. You can smoothen the surface with the aid of a

soft and clean cloth. When you are done, apply a protective finish to the surface of your project.

Skiving Leather

This is the art of reducing the thickness of leather before you adhere two strips of it together. Skiving is mostly done at the edges of the leather to help level the surface. Having a skiving tool can be quite good for a beginner as it helps your projects look even better. The skiving tool is called a skiving knife. A skiving knife will help to ensure an even distribution of the density of leather. Some examples of skiving knives include the following:

- **The leather knife cutting tool**: This tool is a lightweight tool that can be used as both a cutting and an edging knife. It can be used by both beginners and professionals and can be used to skive all densities of leather. The only issue with this tool is that the edges get dulled easily and might need to be sharpened as often as possible.
- **The slanted skiver knife:** This knife is so good that it can work on all weights of leather available with its slanted edge. It can also be used to skive and cut out straight lines on leather. This knife is

easy to sharpen, but then, you might have to spend a lot to purchase it.

Gluing Leather

This process involves you adhering two strips of leather to each other. This technique is one that you must master as a beginner. There are several types of leather glue, but the commonest ones are cement glue and white glue. You should only make use of white glue when seeking temporary bonds that will help you hold the leather as you lace and sew. The cement glue is what you need if you need to permanently join two or more leather strips. Once you work with this glue, you need not sew the joints together again.

Burnishing Leather

This technique is one of the easiest techniques in the art of leather crafting. It is an art of making your leather surface look glossy or shiny by running across it a wooden slicker or burnishing tool. This technique also goes a long way to protect the leather from harsh conditions. Apart from its embellishing touch and protective characteristic, this technique adds a professional touch to your projects.

The kinds of burnishing tools you will find in the market include the hand burnishing tool, or edge slicker, the drill mounted burnishing tool, and the motor-driven burnishing tool. The first type listed here, the edge slicker, has ridges of different sizes in which your leather strips can fit. It is also a handheld tool that you run across your project's edges until you see it become glossy. Fortunately, it is quite cheap and easy to operate.

The drill-mounted burnishing tool will fetch you the same results as the hand burnishing tool, but then, at a much faster rate. This tool, though, is one most professionals opt for when making several projects. To use this tool effectively, you should try getting a few burnishing drill bits. Each of the bits has different widths and can be used for leather of different thickness properties. However, if you plan on using this device as a beginner, ensure that you work at the slowest speed setting at that its mouth presses lightly against the leather surface. Lastly, ensure that the width of the bit you use for your drill is the same as the thickness of your leather strips.

Lastly, the motor burnishing tool, is an electronic device that is powered by a motor. To work with it, you would need to secure it to a workbench with several bolts and screws. This tool is also one of the tools a professional should look forward to getting. At either end of this device are sanding drums, and these things help to sand the two edges of leather strips simultaneously. The process of burnishing with this tool is faster as it finishes in less than ten seconds. To work with this device, just run the leather across the revolving burnishing part. The wonderful thing here is that you can burnish any length of leather easily.

Let's take a quick look at the techniques involves in the burnishing of leather strips.

- **Sanding:** This is the first step you need to execute when burnishing a leather strip. You can work with sandpaper to smoothen the edges of the leather first. This technique will level out the big fibers that bulge out of the regular surface, and also get rid of any glue that remains after adhering two or more strips of leather together. For this process, you can use 200-grit sandpaper or something more technical like a sanding drum.

- **Round the edges with an edge beveller:** An edge beveller is also referred to as an edge shaver, and as a beginner, you could work with the number three or number one sized beveller. This stage works to give your project a nice rounded look and to prevent the edges from gathering up into folds.

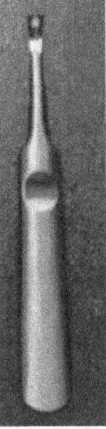

- **Burnishing:** This is the major step involved in burnishing, and it employs friction in the smoothening of the edges of your project. You would notice that after this step, your project would take a darker and smoother look, than when it is not burnished.

There are three methods you can use to get these techniques done though. They include the following:

- **The Water burnish method:** This is one of the most efficient methods of getting the burnishing of leather strips done. You can begin the process by making the edges of the leather strips moist. To do that, spray the edges with a few mists of water. Then, use your slicking tool to stir up friction across the edges by running it across the leather's length. This way, you get to compress the fibers readily. Once you are done with that, you can finish by applying leather edge dye to the edges of the leather strips. You should do that before finishing the burnish so that the dyes can penetrate deeply into the leather fibers. With this method, you could risk making the strips too damp, so, work in bits so that you can easily manage the flow of water. Lastly, this method is very fast and efficient.
- **The wax burnish method:** This technique adds extra layers of smoothness to the edges of leather strips and helps to make your project look even shinier. To work with this method, you just have to follow the steps employed in the method described above. The

only difference is that when you are done, you will need to run a block of beeswax across the burnished edges. After that, you can go on with the step that involves the use of the slicker tool. This method works to protect your project even much more than before, so it's better. The only downside to it is that it needs more brandishing for it to shine.

- **The gum Tragacanth burnish:** This type of gum is also referred to as gum tag, and when it is used for brandishing, it gives the best value to the project. Here also, the basic steps are the same as the ones involved in the water burnish method. After doing all of those, you can finish by adding a thin layer of the gum to the burnished surface. You can add as many layers as you want until you get to a point where your project comes out really smooth and glossy.

When burnishing leather, ensure that you work your tools in the same direction to prevent the disruption of the fibers. Also, when using the water burnish method on vegetable-tanned leather strips, you will need to be very careful to avoid having watermarks on your projects.

Saddle Stitching

This technique involves the art of sewing together strips of leather. You might want to know what this is really about if you don't know how to work with a sewing machine. And surprisingly, the stitches made with this technique is even more durable than the one you make with machines. This durability is because the stitches are done in such a way that they do not loosen even when the thread snaps at its mid-section. This feature is not afforded by the kind of stitches a sewing machine would make.

Now, let's look at a some stitching techniques you would need for your leathercraft projects.

- **Hand-stitching**: There are two types of hand-stitching. There is the single hand-stitching technique and the double hand-stitching technique. However, before you begin to stitch strips of leather together, you must take note of a few things. Cement the leather strip's rough side to the smooth side of the back strip while ensuring that the holes and edges are well aligned. It is also very important to note that the top and the other unpatched parts of the project must not be glued together.

Now, let us study the techniques of hand-stitching.

- Skive one end of the lace with a sharp knife
- Point the skived end of the lace.
- Tug apart the needle's threading end.
- Fix the pointed end of the lace into the needle.
- Close the needle on the lace, and then, tap it lightly with a mallet, so that the prongs can pierce the lace.

- **Whip-stitching**:
  - Thread the needle with the thread
  - Start stitching between the two strips of leather, while still ensuring that about ¼ inch is left at the end where the lace is to be slit.
  - Pass the needle through the second hole, then, through the slit, and finally, through the hole at the opposite end.

- Tug at the stitch to make it tight. Then, continue lacing, while ensuring that you tighten the lace as you move.
- Lace the thread around the project, while making sure to leave a loop in the second hole.
- Lace the thread through the last hole, by passing it between the leathers and the first loop.
- Pullout the first loop over the end of the lace.
- Lastly, pull the end of the lace tightly enough to take the slack out of the last loop. Then, trim off the lace's ends before tapping it flat with the head of a mallet.

Applying Finishes to Leather Strips

Finishes are coats that will help you protect the dyes of your leather strips once they are applied to the length. They will also go a long way to enrich the dye colors of your leather strips as you use them. Some of them are however resistant to water while some aren't. Let's see a few reasons why this technique is equally important.

- Finishing your leather strips will prevent the dyes used in painting the leather from coming in

contact with your skin, especially if your project is something that will be worn close to your body.
- Finishes will help to protect the surface of your leather strips.
- Finishing your projects will give them glossy looks.
- This technique will help enrich the colors used in painting the leather strip.
- It will help add a touch of professionalism to your work, as well as neatness.
- You can prevent the growth of mold on the surface of the leather with this technique.

One kind of finish technique is the idea of burnishing that we discussed earlier above. Then, you could try out techniques like the polishing of the leather strips. The process involves you adding either liquid or solid forms of some substances to the surface of leather. Polishing is something you can do even after years of using your leather projects. However, before you polish your project, ensure that you get rid of the dust and debris that might have accumulated on the surface.

You could also decide to finish your projects by oiling them. Examples of such finish oils include the following:

- Castor oil
- Jojoba oil
- Shea-butter
- Mink oil
- Groundnut oil
- Neat's-foot oil, etc.

Oiling helps prevent your projects from becoming dry or brittle, which means that the presence of ugly cracks along the length can be avoided. Also, the pores of the leather strip will look rich and flexible.

Lastly, let's talk about waxing. This process involves the addition of wax to the surface of leather strips. The wax could either be solid or liquid, but then, the liquid form is mostly preferred as it can penetrate more deeply and quickly into the leather pores. It can also be one method through which the leather maintains its beautiful appearance. Before you begin to wax leather strips though, make sure that the surface is free from dust and debris. Try working with pure wax for this technique, as it will give your work a beautiful appearance.

When waxing your projects, see that you work it into the leather in simple circles. You shouldn't make the coating too thick as you work, and you must ensure that the surface is evenly covered with the wax. You could also work with the aerosol form as you will be able to control the uniformity of the layers this way. Lastly, if you are working with solid wax, you might have to brush the wax across the surface with a soft brush.

Other methods of applying finishes include lacquering, and the addition of antique finishes.

Cleaning and Conditioning Leather

This technique is essential because it will help you keep your leather strips good-looking and nicely textured. To achieve this technique, ensure that you wash the leather with cleaning agents that are mild in nature and help get rid of grime easily. On the other hand, conditioning aims to help the leather strip regain its lost oils and eradicates drying out or cracking of the leather strip.

To clean your leather strips, you can follow the procedures below:

1. Use a clean sponge to apply water to the two sides of your leather project, but then, ensure that it is not so damp that it practically drips of water.
2. Set the leather strip aside until the moisture dries from it. To speed things up, you could use nails or pins to stretch the leather at its edges so that it is properly stretched out. To get the best results, you could wrap the leather with a plastic bag, and then, leave it overnight before you do any other thing on it.
3. If you notice that some areas of the leather strip dried up too quickly, moisten the part again. This technique will make your leather easier to be worked upon by tools.
4. If you accidentally spill water across the entire leather surface, ensure that you moisten the rest of the areas so that whatever color changes are made affects the whole thing.

Stamping

Stamping is possible with the aid of a swivel knife. The following are the different kinds of stamping designs:

- Camouflage
- Pear shade
- Beveller
- Veiner
- Seeder
- Backgrounder
- Veiner stop
- Mules foot
- Basket Stamp.

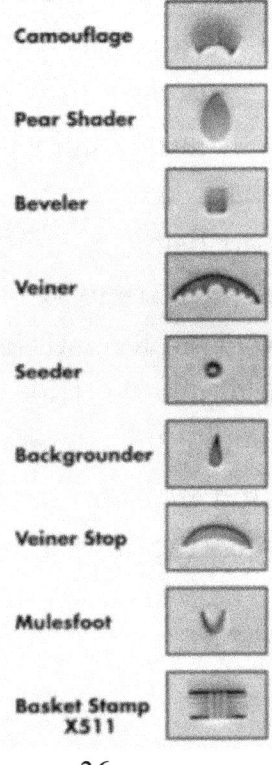

Carving

This process involves the cutting out of the outlines of your designs, and it is made possible with the aid of tools like swivel knives. With it, you can add decorative cuts to your project. You can follow the guidelines below to carve out your design.

- The image below shows the right angle the blade is supposed to make with the swivel knife.
- Keep the side of your hand on the surface of the leather so that the cut is made neatly.
- The more the pressure of the blade you apply on the leather surface, the thicker the lines will be.
- After working with the swivel knife, you can head over to using a camouflage tool. This tool helps to add texture to your design. All you need to do is hold the tool straight up with its mouth pointing downwards. Then, use a mallet to hit the head of the tool down into the leather. To make a different kind of impression on the leather, you can try to alter the angle it makes with it.

As we go further in this text, you will get to know the other carving tools and how they can be used to beautify your projects.

Chapter 3

Leather Crafting Tips and Tricks

Here, we are going to consider the various tips and tricks you can employ when trying out your leather crafts.

1. When using your stamping tool, do not slide it across the surface of the leather. What you ought to do is grip it pretty firmly with one thumb on one side, and with the other fingers grasping it at the other side. Then, use your ring finger to hold down the leather. The tool is meant to just hover slightly above the leather's surface, though.
2. Always keep your swiveling knife sharp and polished, so that it is not being dragged through the pores of the leather. It being dragged through the leather could mean that the tool would be less easy to control.
3. As you use your swivel knife, ensure that you strop it regularly with your jeweler's rouge and cardboard. For the best results, pull the blade back across the rouge towards you. This

technique will help the tool continue to function smoothly.
4. As you cut through your leather, ensure that you turn it around regularly so that you can get a good look at what you are doing. This technique will help you make clean and neat cuts.
5. Practice on scrap leather first before moving ahead to more tangible pieces of leather.
6. Do not use kitchen sponges to dampen your leather because they usually have a build-up of soap particles within them.
7. After dampening your leather strips, ensure that you don't start to work your tools on them immediately. First, wait for the original color of the strips to be regained.
8. You should only dampen the grainy side of your leather strips.
9. If you dampen your leather strips too much, the cuts you make with your swivel knife may not come out too cleanly or intricate enough, and that's not too good.
10. Cuts made on too dry leather strips may not open nicely. Too dry leather strips will make the edge

of your tool drag through the leather, instead of gliding smoothly through it.
11. When dyeing your leather strips, start at the center of the project, and then, let the color drip to the other parts.
12. To give your projects a glossy and beautiful appearance, coat their surfaces with several layers of wax, or any other finish. You should also ensure that you wipe off the dust from the surfaces before applying the finishes.
13. To work more effectively with a veiner, tilt it towards the left or right side, depending on the direction the design heads towards. Then, use a mallet to strike it down for effect.
14. When working with a mule's foot, tilt it forward, and then, hit it deeply to make a deep impression. Applying a decreasing pressure on the tool will help create a nice effect on your project.
15. You should plan out your decorative cuts before you follow through with them. That technique will help your designs to be accentuated in the right places.

16. There are different kinds of swivel blades available. Only work with the ones that work best for you.

A Short message from the Author:

Hey, I hope you are enjoying the book? I would love to hear your thoughts!

Many readers do not know how hard reviews are to come by and how much they help an author.

I would be incredibly grateful if you could take just 60 seconds to write a short review on Amazon, even if it is a few sentences.

>> Click here to leave a quick review

Thanks for the time taken to share your thoughts!

Chapter 4

Getting Started with Leather Crafting

Leather Crafting Tools and Supplies

Leather Material

Forms of Leather

Before we go into the details, you need to first understand what tanning means. It is the process by which animal skin or hide is converted into something tougher and stronger.

1. **Vegetable-tanned leather:** This type of leather is one that has been tanned with tannic acid, a chemical derived from trees, and plants. This kind of leather will readily bear any design you make on it by either carving or stamping. Also, once you get this kind of leather moistened, it is possible to mold it into any shape of your choice.

It can hold any form you mold it to even moments after it has dried.

2. **Mineral or Chrome tanning:** Here, the animal hides are tanned with potassium dichromate. This kind of leather is usually soft to touch, easy to ply with tools, and water-resistant. Its water resistance is what makes it unsuitable for carving or stamping. After cutting strips out of this kind of leather, the edges usually turn a bluish-green color, and that is caused by the minerals that were used in the tanning process. This kind of leather can be used to produce clothes, furniture, upholstery, and other projects that require soft and durable leather.

3. **Oil-tanned leather:** This procure involves the usage of oils to tan leather strips with dark hues. Leather that is tanned with this method can be easily rolled into bundles, without creasing the leather too much. Also, when a leather that is tanned with this method is creased, the crease lines come out lighter than the color of the whole leather. You could also employ the contrast in oil-tanned leather strips for pouches, satchels, and bags.

Quality and Grades of Leather

- **Full-grain leather**: This kind of leather is obtained from the outer part of the animal skin, and it happens to be the strongest and most durable kind of leather that you can ever get. Along with the entire hide, you can be sure to find the strongest fibers. Another good thing about this kind of leather is that it can stand the test of time. It neither wears out nor breaks down with time, and, it can be used to make the most beautiful projects. However, because of its beautiful features, it can be very expensive to get. So, before you work with it, make sure that you have practiced severally on other cheaper leather types.
- **Top-grain leather:** This kind of leather is easy to get, and that makes it a whole lot cheaper. Here, the leather's surface has been sanded to get rid of the uppermost grains. These uppermost grains are responsible for the strength, and durability of the leather, so, since they are scraped away, this leather becomes less durable.

- **Genuine leather:** This kind of leather is one that occurs most readily, and can be bought at the cheapest prices. The leather is smooth and free from the marks of grains. So, know that any grain mark you see on it is more of an artificial impression.

Types of Leather

1. **Buffalo leather**
- It comes from the Asian Buffalo
- The hide can be about 40 square feet long
- It has the bovine characteristic of cowhide.
- The grains of this leather is grainy, just like that of pigskin.
- You can use this kind of leather for shoes, boots, and smaller leather projects.

2. **Calfskin**
- It is obtained from a young bovine insides or whole hide.
- Its length is about 18 square feet.
- The grain lines are tightly packed together, with a collective fine texture.

- This kind of leather is good for shoes, boots, and leather projects that require smoothness.

3. **Cowhide**
- This is the commonest and most versatile leather.
- It is tanned insides of 18 to 24 square feet.
- It is very durable and can be easily worked with.
- Cowhide can be about 16 ounces thick, whether it is vegetable or chrome-tanned.
- It is used for making furniture, footwear, saddles, tack, and belts.

4. **Deerskin**
- This kind of leather is tanned in whole hides of about 7 to 12 square feet.
- It has a soft and elastic structure.
- It is very light.
- The property above is what makes it suitable for use in the production of gloves, moccasins, and garments.

5. **Goatskin**
- This one is tanned in thin and small whole hides.
- It is relatively tough and durable.
- It is finished in different bright colors.

- It can be used for making women's shoes and the top of cowboy boots.

6. **Kangaroo**
- This leather is thin, and light.
- It can stand the test of time.
- It is very strong, even stronger than the other types of leather.
- The whole skin is about five to seven square feet long.
- It can be used for producing soccer shoes, sports gloves, or as thin strips used for lacing and braiding.

7. **Pigskin**
- This exists as whole hides, and they are about ten to twenty feet square long.
- They have a coarse grain texture.
- They are usually embossed with another texture to hide their coarse grains.
- They can be used as garment leather, lining leather, shoe linings, garments, and other small leather projects.

8. **Reptile**

- This leather is gotten from snakes, lizards, alligators, and crocodiles.
- It is available in different grains and textures.
- It is very rare and valuable.
- It can be used for making fancy leather projects, boots, shoes, belts, wallets, and handbags.

9. **Sheepskin**
- This leather is light and delicate.
- When it is tanned, it comes out really soft.
- It is usually tanned alongside wool.
- It can be used for making coats, car upholstery, and saddle lining.

Working Surface

This one is also known as the cutting surface. You can work with either hardened rubber or polyethylene. The board will help shield the surface of your work and help keep the edges of your cutting tool sharp.

Sewing Thread

This thread is used to adhere two strips of leather together. The type of thread you use is determined by the thickness of the leather you are sewing, as well as the strength of the stitches you want your project to have.

Pencils, Paper, and Cardboard

These materials are utilized at the beginning of the project when drawing out the outlines of the design to be used. The outlines are first drawn on the paper, after which they are cut out from it and fixed to the surface of the cardboard with the aid of rubber glue.

Straight-Edged Ruler or Steel Square

These tools are used for measuring the dimensions of your patterns, and the outlines of your designs. They are also important tools used in the cutting out of straight lines in leather. For your leatherwork projects, ensure that you do not use rulers that haven't been painted or finished moderately, as their metallic structure can stain your leather. Instead, go for the ones made out of aluminum, plastic, or wood.

Scratch Awl

This tool is used for marking out the structure of cutting to be used for a leather project. It helps to mark out points where holes, snaps, rivets, stitches, and laces should be in. You can use an awl that has a sharp edge for this purpose. But then, whenever you aren't using it, ensure that you cover the edge with a rubber guard.

Knife and Leather Shears

These tools are used for cutting out the design patterns on leather. For most of the leatherwork projects, you could use either utility knives or box knives. For a sharp cutting edge, using a snap-off blade is much more preferable. Craft knives are only good for projects where the leather is light-weight. Leather shears, on the other hand, are good for cutting out leather strips that are to be used for making garments. However, the kind of cuts they make can never be as accurate as the ones a sharp knife would make.

Rubber Cement and White Glue

These are used for making patterns. Rubber cement is however easier to wipe off the surface of a material.

Latex Gloves

You will need this to shield your hands from dangerous chemicals while working on leather projects.

Strap Cutter

This tool can be used to cut leather into straps used for making belts of different widths, dog collars, or any other thing in that fashion. Straps can also be cut out with knives and rulers, but then, a strap cutter only makes the process a lot easier, especially for making belts or any other related projects on a large scale.

Tracing Film

This is a plastic or polyester film that works like tracing paper would. You use this film to transfer design outlines to the surface of leather. Tracing paper could also perform the same function, but then, we wouldn't advise that you get it because it is not as durable as the tracing film. Tracing films can be reused several times after the first time.

Modeling Tools

You should use the pointed edge of this tool to move design outlines from tracing films to leather. The spoon edge of this tool is the part that should be used to shape out and smoothen the creases on leather.

Brushes or Wool Daubers

You can use these tools to apply pigments like dyes, stains, and finishes to the surface of leather.

Water Container, Sponge, and Spray Bottles

These tools are used for making leather damp before you begin to use your tools on them for carving, molding, or stamping. The water container should be made with either plastic, glass, porcelain, or enamel. Never use a metallic container as the water stored within it will stain the surface of the leather. To apply the water to the surface of the leather, you could either use the sponge or a spray bottle.

Tooling Surface

This surface is what you need when tooling and stamping leather strips. It must be hard and very smooth. You could go for one made with marble, but then, granite or a pressed hardboard will also do the trick. The surface should be about 1 to 2 inches dense, and the general dimensions should be about 6-by-12-by-12-inches. It would be much better if the surface were mobile too. A cutting mat made with toughened rubber may be fixed to one side of the stone to reduce the noise made while stamping.

Swivel Knife

This tool can be used to cut out design outlines on leather surfaces. It has a finger rest located at the side opposite the swiveling structure of the blade. The swivel technique works by making the blade easier to control as it works its way through the leather surface.

Metal Stamping Tools

These tools are used to make decorative impressions on the surface of leather. Each stamping tool has a kind of impression it makes, and that is what makes one different from the other. To create a design, you only need one stamping tool, but for more complicated designs, you might need several stamping tools at the same time.

Mallet

This tool is used for striking the tools you use for stamping, punching, and other techniques in the art of leather crafting. The head of the mallet is usually constructed from either hide, polyethylene, or wood. However, you will never hear of it being made of metal. You know, if you strike a metallic tool with a metalhead, you can be sure of destroying that tool.

Edge Beveller

This tool is used to bevel, trim, and round-off the edges of leather. This technique will fetch your projects a more professional look. And this tool is available in different sizes. The smaller the number of the bevel, the smaller the bevel will be. For most of the leatherwork projects, you will need a size 2 beveller.

Hole Punches

This tool is used for punching holes into the surface of leather, and for punching holes that would be employed in the stitching and the lacing of materials.

There are two types of hole punches. One is the single-drive punch that punches a single hole the moment you strike its head with a mallet. Ensure that you place a rubber cutting board under the leather before you punch holes through it with a single-drive punch. The other type is the pliers-type punch. This one punches a hole through a leather material when you squeeze it like you would do a pair of pliers. These kinds of punches can either have a single-sized tube or about six various sizes of tubes that you can mount on a rolling wheel.

Setters

This tool is used for setting snaps and rivets in leather projects like belts, pouches, sheaths, etc.

Pear Shader

This tool is used to shape the areas outlined by a swivel knife. It forms low spots and high spots on the surface of the leather, thereby, giving it a more natural look. To use it, hold it straight up with the tip pointing downwards. Then, use a hammer to push it down. Repeat this procedure throughout the leather.

Veiner

This tool is used to add veins to leaves and for creating some other striking effects. The angle at which you work this tool determines the length of the cut it makes through the leather.

Seeder

This tool is used for making seed pods at the center of the flower. This tool is much smaller than the other tools, so it doesn't really need much pressure applied on it for it to make an impression on leather.

Setting Up Your Leather Crafting Workshop

This stage is another of the very salient things you need to consider before setting off to crafting any leather. Any mistake here can lead to safety hazards, and you surely do not want that to happen. So, follow the steps here to set up your workshop in a safe manner.

1. Use a sturdy table with a regular surface that is free from bumps and dents.
2. Work in a room with lots of light. If the natural sun rays cannot find their way into your workspace, then, you should get fluorescent lamps that you can fix to the ceiling. The more of

these lights that you have in your workshop, the easier it is for you to do intricate things like the cutting out of outlines on leather.
3. Your workspace must be well-ventilated.
4. The chair you desire to sit on as you work on your project must be high enough to make your hands above the table. This way, your head, and arms do not have to be elevated at an uncomfortable angle when crafting out your projects.
5. Reserve areas that will hold tools for design and transfer (pencils, tracing film, cardboard, glue) cutting and assembly (scissors, blade, punches, chisels, rulers, glue), stamping and carving (plastic bowl, spray water bottle, mallet), coloring and finishing (dyes, stains, finishes, sponge, soft cloth) and lastly, first aid (mild soap, bandages). This technique will prevent the tools from getting mixed up as you work.

Leather Crafting Safety Measures

The art of leather crafting involves the use of several tools that have very sharp cutting edges. These tools are grouped under the following categories;

- Pushed tools like gouges, skivers, and a few knives.
- Pulled tools like swivel knives, utility knives, and strap cutters.
- Struck tools like paper and leather punches, chisels, etc.

Now, the following measures below will help you remain safe even as you carry out the art of leather crafting.

1. You need to make sure that the blades of the tools listed above are sharp enough to make clean cuts through your leather strips. Dull cutting blades can be very dangerous for your projects.
2. Grip your tools firmly as you use them so that they don't go beyond the points they are meant to work on.
3. Never position any part of your body along the path a cutting tool will follow.

4. Leather crafting has a lot of things to do with materials like dyes, cement glues, and all sorts of finishes, so you should ensure that you work in a room with cross-ventilation. Also, before you use any chemical, check the labels for the manufacturer's guide, and follow any instructions you are given there.
5. Never allow the chemicals listed above to come in contact with your skin, as they can be pretty harsh. To ensure this, wear gloves whenever you work with the chemicals.
6. To prevent the chemicals from spilling over, ensure that you replace their lids whenever you are done.
7. Never work with any of the chemicals—finishes, glue, and dyes—near open flames.
8. Always have a first aid box around in case of any emergency.
9. If you end up cutting yourself lightly with the cutting blade of any tool, quickly wash the wound with mild soap and water to prevent germs from getting into it. Then, apply an antiseptic on it to protect it from infections. Lastly, keep the wound covered!

10. For deeper cuts, immediately apply pressure to the wound to control the bleeding. After that, clean the wound however way you can so that it doesn't get infected. Use a sterile gauze pad and tape to cover the wound.
11. If you notice that your skin gets irritated each time you use a particular chemical, wash the spot with mild soap and water. Then, get checked at a hospital to prevent it from growing into an issue much worse.
12. Keep your mouth closed as you work with chemicals to prevent poisoning.

Chapter 5

Leathercraft Project Ideas

Leather Cat Purse

A fashionable purse to keep your personal belongings in. You can use two different colors of material to make your leather purse. it's a purse with cat features (eyes, whiskers, ears)

Supplies

- Two different colors of leather to make the body of the purse
- Black and pink leather for the face and ears of the cat (you can use any other color, but black and pink is perfect for this)
- Zipper(10cm long)
- Fabric scissors
- Adhesive glue
- A purse chain
- Big and small binder clips
- Ruler
- Rotary cutter
- Sewing machine
- Brown paper
- Stiffener

Procedures

1. Use a ruler to mark 9 cm wide circle from the brown paper to make the front of your cat face. To make the back piece, place the already cut-out pattern on another brown paper piece, then cut out your back piece. Now you have two cuts out from your brown paper to use as a template on your leather.

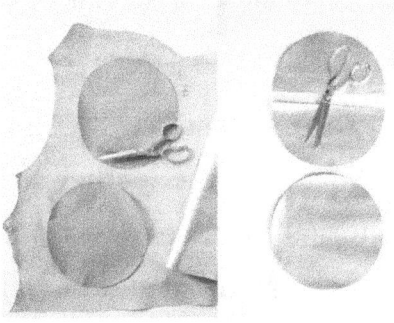

2. To make a seam allowance for your zipper, take the paper for the back piece from the circle's center, measure 1mm on the left side and 1mm on the right side. Trace each marked side with dotted lines. Also, rule a straight line in the center. Cut your circle into

half along the dotted lines. Ensure you cut along the dotted lines to give space for seaming allowance and so that it can form a whole circle after the zip is sewn into it. Trace your front and back piece on your leather's back; use scissors to cut out your shape.

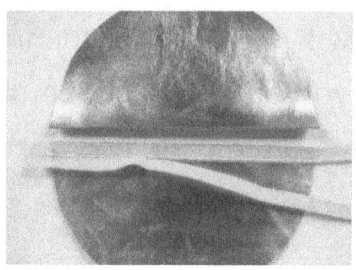

3. Repeat the process to attach the zipper's left side in place and sew across the leather from the zipper so that the seam allowance doesn't bulge. Zip your circle up and measure it against the front side of your circle; if it's not equal, you can trim the part that is more than the other, so both sides can even up.

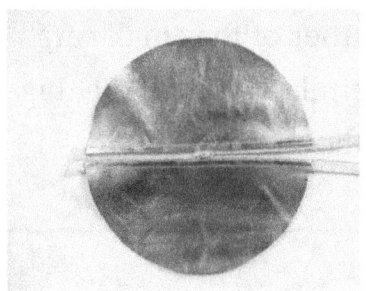

4. Make a paper triangle pattern for your ear that is 3cm long at the bottom and 2cm high. Add an extra 1 inch to each bottom to become short after gluing it to your purse. Cut out four cat-shaped ears from the leather of your choice, two big ears from the first colour of the leather and two small ears from the other leather for the inside of your ears. You don't need to add extra inches to the smaller ears.

5. Glue the smaller ears onto the top of two of your main leather ears. Let the glue dry. Sew the outer

part of the leather of the small ears with your sewing machine carefully. Attach the big ears with glue right behind the small ears.

6. Using your ruler and a rotary cutter, cut a strand of leather that is 28 long and 11/4 wide to make room for sewing allowance.
7. Turn the leather strand to the wrong side, mark the middle point of it, make long lines from the center of this leather that your ears will be fixed, affix a hole for the chain at the end of where each ear will be fixed. To make the chain rope attached, cut two small strips of leather that are ¼ inches wide and 2 inches long for the purse chain hole. Place the strips across each other, then sew across the middle of the folded strip to make a loop at the top.

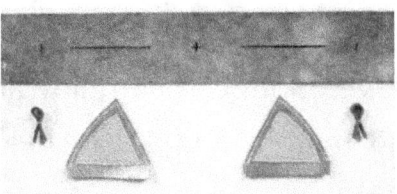

8. Move your ears up through each slit until you get to the downside that has not been sewn. Open up the ear flap against the bottom of the leather. Cut out and fasten in place with glue, repeat the process for the left ears.

9. Make sure the flaps are straightened out against each other and glued in place.
10. To prevent the shape from giving in from weight or pressure, fasten with glue, a strip bag stiffener to the inside of the strip we cut out earlier. Use the same measurement that was used to cut out the strip to cut out the bag stiffener that is (28 inches long and 11/4 inches wide).

11. Attach with glue onto the bottom of the strip so that you still have enough seam allowance, ¼ inches at the top and bottom and 1/2 inches on the left and right sides.
12. To keep your strip inside out, fix the two ends that have your 1/2" seam allowance and sew them together. Ensure the seam is flattened out the way the zipper was flattened out while sewing so they don't bulge.

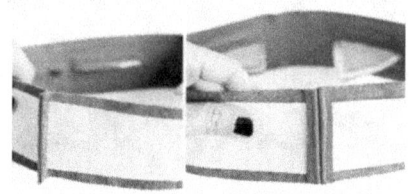

13. Make the inside of the purse after you have made the outer part. Pick up the front circle we cut at the beginning and place it face down on top of your outside grey circle. Use small binder clips to carefully line up the edges of your outside and front pieces, glue with the adhesive glue and clip the edges in place. Once the glue is dry, detach some of

the clips and put the zipper foot back on your sewing machine. Sew near the 1/4" seam allowance and carefully along the bag stiffener. Don't rush while sewing it so it doesn't get stuck to the machine's teeth plate. Flatten the part that is about to be sewn by the machine at a time. Don't worry about the stiffener creasing. It will bounce outback.

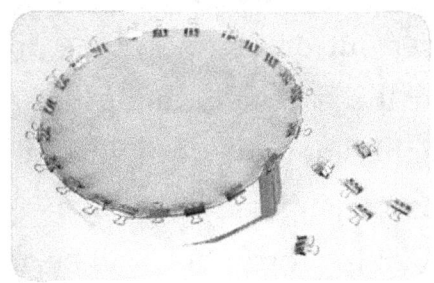

14. After you have sewn the stiffener and the inside, repeat the gripping process with clip and gluing with an adhesive on the backside of your bag. Ensure your zipper edges are trimmed, and the zip is placed straight horizontally at the back of the bag. Unzip it a bit to use your finger to turn it right side out once you are done.

15. This last step might be difficult to sew because the bag has both sides sewn into it, in addition to the bag stiffener. Don't let that bother you; keep flattening the stiffener out one bit at a time. Immediately you have fixed the backside, unzip the zipper and turn the bag right side out. It might bring a feeling that you are destroying the bag stiffener in the process; however, not to worry. You will be amazed that they will still come out in the right shape.

16. Turn the bag inside out, then apply or glue some eyes, nose, mouth, whiskers to make it look like a real kitty bag. In the end, you have something like this.

Leather Tassel Sandals

Tassels made from leather adds a unique touch to your sandal heels.

Supplies
- Strappy sandals
- Two colors of different leather fabric
- Fabric adhesive (glue)
- Fabric scissors
- Ruler
- Pencil or pen

Procedures

1. Pick leather fabrics that compliment each other when placed on your sandals. Cut up each piece equally.

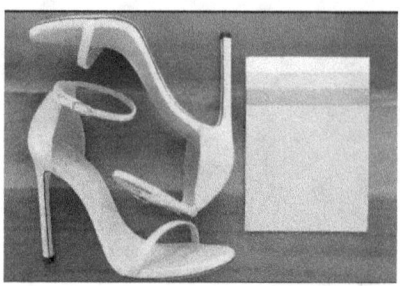

2. Place your ruler across the fabric's length, leave about 1/2 space, then draw a straight line. Repeat the process on the remaining leather.

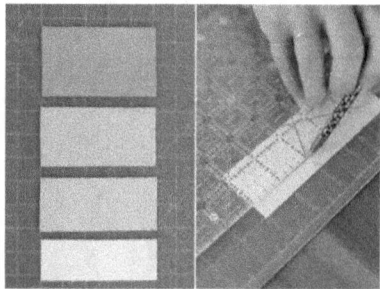

3. Cut your fabric into tiny pieces with scissors. Do not cut beyond the straight line. Demarcate where you are to cup up to. Do the same on other pieces.

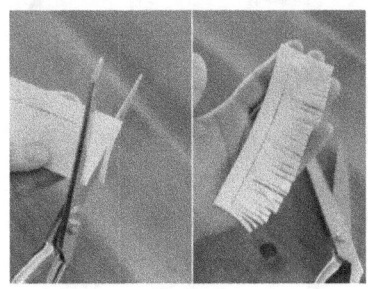

4. Drip a little quantity of glue on the tip of each tiny pieces.
5. Use the far end of the fabric to close the line to form a loose hole. Make the loophole stand right above the line of the fringe.

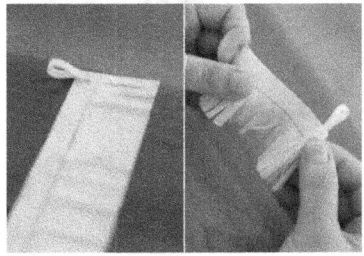

6. When you reach the end of the fringe, drip a little quantity of glue at the end of the top to form a sealed fringe

7. Leave your tassels to dry for about one to two hours before putting them into the straps of your sandals.

Leather Earrings

Supplies

- Leather(a different set of leathers)
- Leather punch

- Sharp scissors
- Two big jump rings
- Two earring wires
- Jewelry pliers

Procedures

1. Draw out these different sizes of shapes on a craft paper, place it on your leather and cut out two pairs of each size.

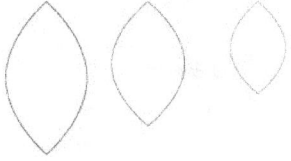

2. Place a set of the three shapes on each other. Cautiously punch a hole on one of the ends. Repeat with the second set of leather.

3. With a plier, attach the jump ring through the leather set and attach the earring to the wearing wire. Repeat this step with the second group of leather.

Leather Valet Tray

Keeping your items in a valet tray prevents you from turning the whole house upside down to find the item. It's the perfect place to keep your glasses, car keys, debit and credit cards, etc.

Supplies

- Leather scrap
- Copper rivets
- Copper burrs
- Ruler
- Marking tool (pen, awl, or embosser)
- Ball peen hammer and/or rivet setter
- Knife
- Hole punch (optional)

Procedures

1. Mark the outside shape of the valet, as well as the lines where you will end up folding the leather up to mark the sides. Use a pen that doesn't have the ink runny to avoid smearing your leather with ink. Then, cut out the leather with a knife.
2. After that, fold the leather across the carved line to hold the desired shape when the corners are pinched up towards each other.

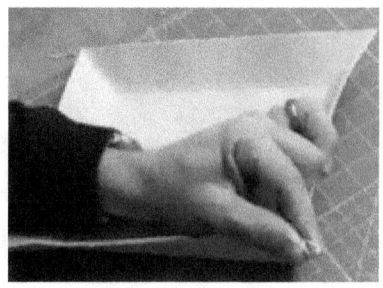

3. Raise the leather's four corners together, secure them in place. Use rivets to sew them together. However, if you can't use rivets, use needle and thread, or a tool you are familiar with that can do the job like a speedy stitcher.
4. Figure out where to place the rivets. Just remember, the rivets will actually raise and hold the leather together about (1/8 inch) beyond the edge of the rivet head. To fix the rivers, you can buy an extra rivet and practice with them on the leftover pieces.

7. After fixing the rivets in their holes, hit them extremely hard into the hole so they don't come off easily.

Leather Flannel Snap Scarf

A leather piece with snaps is sewn along the edge of a flannel scarf. Flannel is a cotton-made material. It is cozy and fluffy to the touch. You are probably bored of the trade of wounding around your neck a flannel scarf. You should try to fix a leather piece at the edge and make snaps on them. With the snaps, you don't have to bother about your scarf twirling around your neck. Below are what you need to make a leather Flannel Snap Scarf.

Supplies

- 1 Soft leather trim piece
- 5 Dritz Western Heavy Duty Snaps
- Heavy Duty Snap Tool for attaching
- Schmetz leather sewing machine needle
- Flannel fabric: about 1 1/4 yards
- Matching Thread
- Sewing machine
- Scissors

- Ruler
- Hand sewing needle
- Pins and clover clips

Procedure

1. Prepare your flannel fabric
- Fold your fabric into two. Ensure that the patterns are folded in symmetrical lines, so they match up when the two pieces are sewn together. You certainly don't want to go about with two different pieces that their patterns do not match.

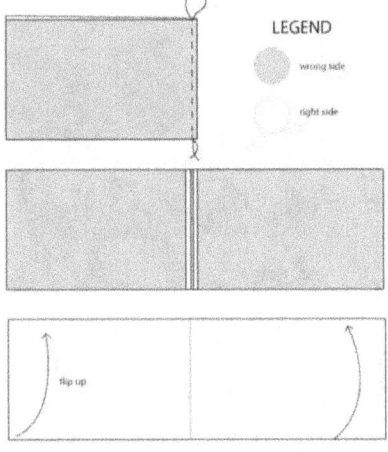

- Hold the two right sides, pin the two pieces at the short ends and add 1/2 space for sewing allowance. Make sure the length and width of the left and right sides are equal. None should be longer than the other. If you think an 11/4 material will give you head shape while cutting, you can go for 2½ yard of the fabric.

2. Prepare leather snap packet.

- So you don't cut less than the piece, you need to cut the leather into equal halves. Pin the flannel piece together at the edges. Ensure the folded piece matches.

3. Remove the pins fixed at the ends, flip the first layer of your flannel piece and place the leather

piece at the end. Ensure the edges of the leather trim are symmetrical with the edges of the flannel not to shift when sewing. Clip the ends with clover clips. Give ½ space above the beginning of the leather and cut-out piece and the long raw edges of the fabric for sewing allowance. Use the needle for sewing leathers to sew all edges, sewing threads for cloth won't hold the leather together with the material, so it's better to use sewing wool for leather. Don't forget to sew with the ½ allowance else, the leather flannel won't turn out well.

4. Leave three inches opening unsewn in the center of the scarf for easy turning. Don't forget to stitch at the beginning and end of the Gap, so the

thread doesn't loosen up. Stitching prevents the cloth from tearing out easily

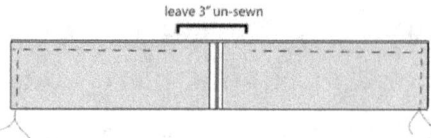

5. Use a pair of scissors to trim out the corners. Be careful not to cut beyond the stitches.
6. Use a pen or blunt pencil to tune out the cloth through the unseamed part. Use an iron to straighten out the flannel. Do not iron the leather.
7. Sew the unseamed part manually with a needle and thread.

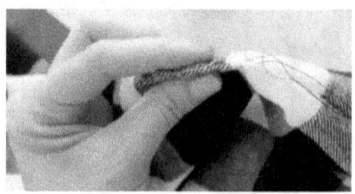

8. Measure out where the snap will be placed. Install snaps across the marked placed. Make sure the opened part is against the enclosed part.

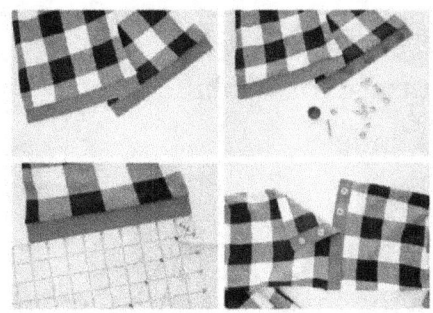

Voila! Your leather flannel is ready for use!

Leather Tablet Case

Supplies

- Leather

- Suede Lining
- A wooden mallet
- a hard surface for tooling
- A swivel knife
- Stencil beveling tool
- Ruler and fabric shears
- Fasteners for snap
- A setter for locking the parts together
- A hole punch tool
- Needles for sewing leather
- Waxed thread for sewing leather
- Awl is needed to drill holes into leather
- A Creasing Tool - to even the lines on the edge before sewing.
- Overstitch wheel - to mark where the snaps will be attached.
- Craftool Stitching Groover. (This gouges a channel along the edge to prepare it for the holes & sewing)
- Leather glue
- Satin Sheen

Procedures

1. Cut out and Shape the Leather. Use the size of your device to cut out the size and shape of your tablet. You don't need to use a piece of leather. You can use different types to make it. If you are using two different pieces, cut out the leather piece.
- Then use an edge tool to even out the creases.

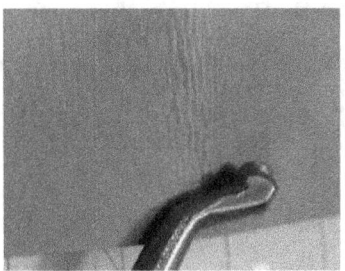

- Spray it to make it soft and easy to fold into your desired shape. Leave to dry.

- After it has dried, cut out a lapel piece from the remaining material.

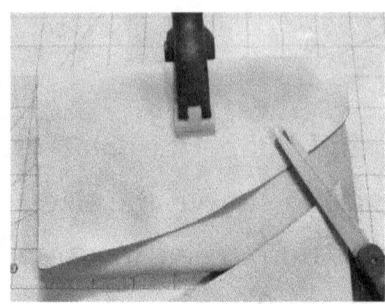

- Then sew the pieces together, line them up, and spray them with water. Use an adhesive to stick one piece of the leather to the other. Leave to dry for about 25 minutes.
- After it has dried, spread water on the leather to get it a bit wet, use the creasing tool to chisel it out, use a stitching groover to cut out a line for seaming, and make marks for holes use an overstitch wheel.
- Create holes using an awl on both materials to allow for stitches.

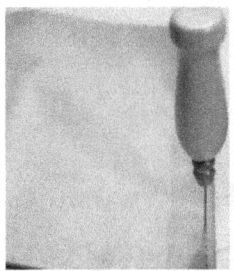

- You can use your hand to sew the materials together if you do not have a stitching machine.

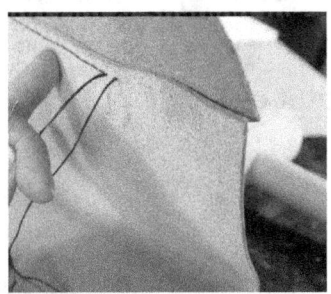

- Reshape the leather. Even though you had done that earlier, it could have
lost its shape due to stitching, so you need to redo it again. Spread water
over the leather, wrap it with a book or something close to your tablet's shape to cake out the shape, remember to put a cover over the

leather so it doesn't have marks from creasing objects.

2. Tooling the Feather. You can use any tooling you like. However, in this book, we will make use of a stencil to tool out the feather.
- Place the stencil on your dampened leather. Use a spoon, knife, or any object that can smoothen the stencil you want to appear on the leather.
- Once you have placed it on the leather, trace the lines and cut it out.

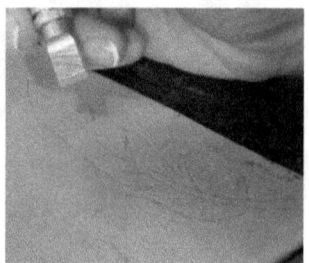

- Should in case the leather dries out, dampen it again. Take out a beveling tool and your mallet and start by going around the outside edge lines with the tool. Gently hit the edge lines with the mallet and push it along the line bit by bit. Move it till you are done; repeat the same process for the lines inside.

3. Line your leather with suede.

- Carve out the piece of suede and glue it to the inside of the leather case.

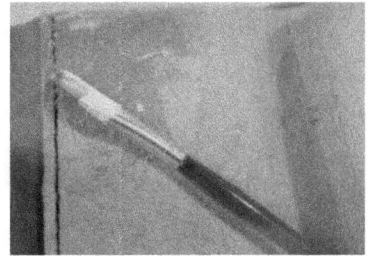

- Use a brush to get the glue spread evenly on the inside of the case and on the one side of the suede that will be attached inside. Leave it to dry a bit. Take the slightly dried and sticky leather case, place the suede inside the leather case, and smoothen it all out very fast. Once dry, trim off any excess suede.

4. Adding the inside pieces to secure the tablet

- You have to be precise and careful when carrying out this step. Position the tablet into the center area, shut the case to get a feel for exactly where the tablet should be placed. Then, put a few pins into the suede to create a border where the tablet should be positioned, so you know where to put the little corner holders. You need to cut out pieces for the holder at the corners.

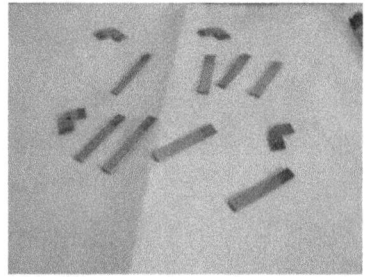

- Considering the type of tablet you are making the leather case tablet for, you need to cut out pieces for the holders. The holders may be at the corner.

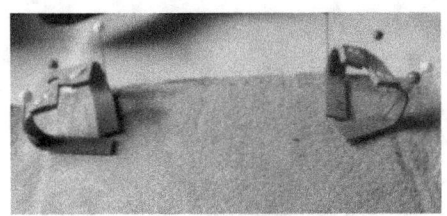

- Where the speaker of the phone is, there should be a cut-out. Use glue to hold the pieces together. Wet the leather and use the awl to pierce holes into the little pieces. After all pieces are sewn together, wet them again. When you let them dry, they will shape out properly. Once dry, remove them one-by-one, let the bottom strips be above each other and use the awl to punch holes. Punch holes in the right space on the main leather piece and secure the small pieces to the main leather case by sewing them together in three different spots.
- Work on the corner piece, one after the other, measure it as you work on it to ensure the tablet will fit in the right place. You certainly don't want your tablet sticky and out of balance in its case.

5. Adding the snap enclosure

1. Locate the spot where you want to add it, center it as much as possible, and make a small mark. Repeat the same process for the bottom part of your bottom snap to line up with the first top. After doing so, dampen the leather with glue and make a hole with a rotary hole punch.

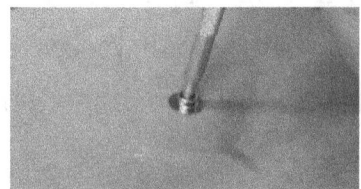

2. Most snap kits come with an instruction guide book. Place the top snap with the flattened metal piece with the leather in between. To fix the top snap with the flat metal piece, ensure the small

metal anvil piece goes beneath it. Then use a craft-tool setter and the mallet to fix the pieces together to lock them in.

3. The top piece will have the metal anvil, then the cap, which has the top shooting out through the leather loop, then the socket. Once you are done adding the snap enclosure, the image below is supposed to look.

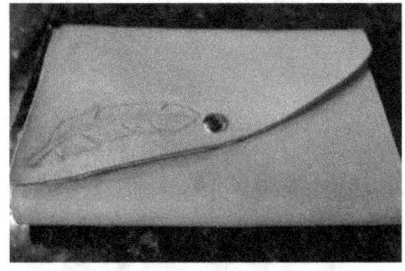

6. Dying & Finishing the Leather With a Satin Sheen

4. For the leather to look brighter, smooth, and beautiful, use a satin sheen for the finishing.

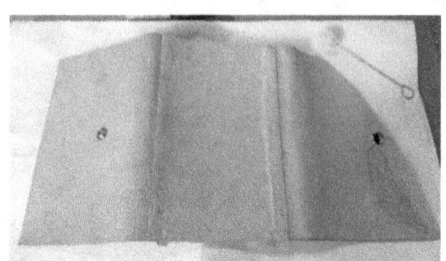

5. Before you dye your leather, it is advised to clean the leather with alcohol or deglazer. After, leave it to dry. While it's drying, put on a pair of disposable gloves, and test the dye on a piece that is not useful before trying it out on your leather case.

6. Apply the dye evenly with a soft cloth or foam. Allow it to dry.

7. After it has dried, use your satin sheen over it to make it shine. With the gloves on, use foam to apply the sheen on the case. When you're done, your leather case will be looking shiny and beautiful.

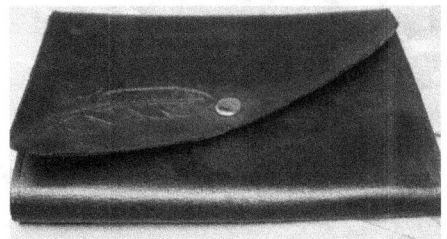

Leather Camera Strap

If your camera strap gets weak or old, you can replace them with a leather camera strap. Leathers are more durable than the material used for the belt of your camera. Here's what you need to make a leather camera strap.

Supplies

- A piece of leather that is 4.5 inches wide and 24 inches long
- Clothespins
- Embroidery or seam ripper
- Scissors
- Leather needle
- A thread that matches the color of your leather strap
- An old camera strap

Procedures

1. With your seam ripper, loosen the bottom of your original strap. You can use an embroidery ripper if you cannot access a seam ripper.

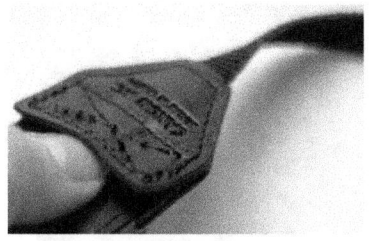

2. Straighten the length out to form a perfect angle on the side. Place your ruler in a straight line from the curve on the side and then mark it with a pen or pencil, then carve it out with fabric scissors.

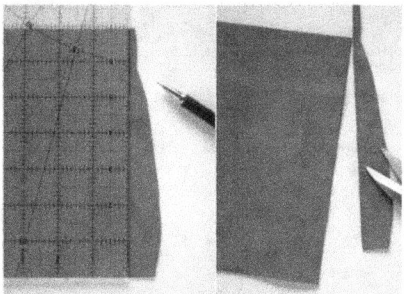

3. Your strap should be 1.5cm. In other to cut this measurement out, you need to fold your leather three times. Using a ruler, draw out an even edge and cut your leather into the strap size.

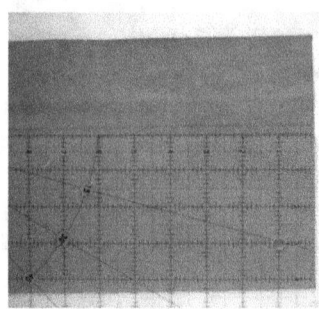

4. Use your ruler and pencil to draw horizontal lines across the length of the leather strip of 1.5 from the top.

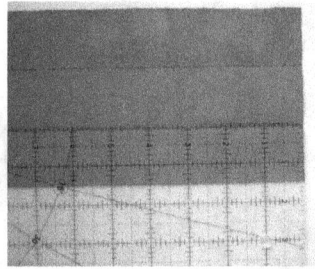

5. Fold your leather and clip with a cloth pin.

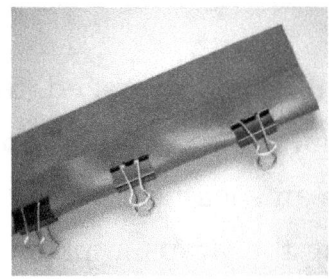

6. When about to sew, roll a thread that matches your leather on the reeler of your machine. Ensure you stitch the edge of the folded side of the strip. To give it a professional look and make it easy to loosen if you make any mistake, use a big stitch.
7. Leave equal seam allowance on the edge and the folded side of your strip. Clip to hold in place and sew along the edges of the three layers of leather you had cut out.

8. Turn the leather to the first edge and topstitch 1/4 from the first seam. Do the same for the second edge of the same leather.
9. After sewing the straps in place, take the original strap bases and put the leather strap between them. If the original strap got spoilt while ripping, you could get an adjustable strap at the store. Use something to hold it in place, then sew through all the layers, tracing the X and rectangle stitching of the original leather strap. Repeat on the second side.

10. Done! Your camera strap is smooth and ready for use!

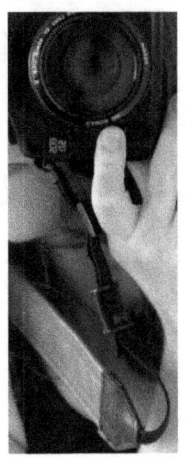

Leather Clutch Bags

Leather clutch bags are super stylish bags that help you carry your small gadgets, make-up materials, keys, money, and the likes. They are stylish in the sense that they effortlessly blend well with your stunning outfits, making you look peng while carrying the clutch bag. It is essential to have a leather clutch bag in cases where you need to go out quickly, but you don't want to carry something heavy on your hands or shoulders. Having a leather clutch bag will help you in this predicament. Making a leather clutch bag is very easy, and as a DIY enthusiast, you will breeze through this project by following these procedures!

Note: You can make your leather clutch bags into different sizes depending on what you want to use them to carry.

Supplies

- A leather material
- Brass stud screw backs
- Printed cotton fabric
- Fusible applique paper
- A small-sized template
- A large-sized template
- Leather hole punch
- A Sharp scissors

Procedures

1. First, you need to print out your template. If you make a small leather clutch bag, trace out your

template using the measurements (3.5 x 5) inches on your leather's backside. For a large envelope clutch bag, trace out your template using the measurements (4.5 x 6) inches.

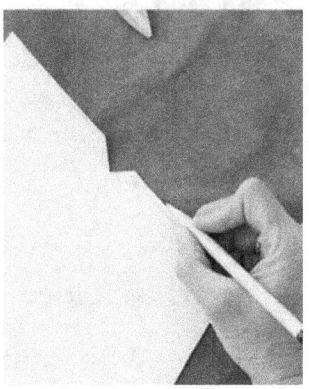

2. Print out two copies of your template. Cut them out and tape them together. (Ensure that you cut the template to the paper edge when pruning).

Next, you will have to cut out the clutch bag shape made from the template on your leather. Be very careful not to cut the critical side of your leather. You can make use of your scissors to cut it out.

3. After you cut it out, mark a spot on the corners of your leather where the hole punch will go. Make the area accurate as you want the punctured holes to match up when folded together.

Once you are done with that, get your fabric ready for lining the inside of your clutch material.

4. Next, you will trace the portion of the top of the envelope onto the back (wrong) side of the fabric using your template. After, remove a side of the fusible applique paper and then place it on the backside of your fabric and iron them together.

5. Place the sticky side of your fusible applique paper to the inside of your leather clutch and iron them together. (Make sure that you iron using low heat).

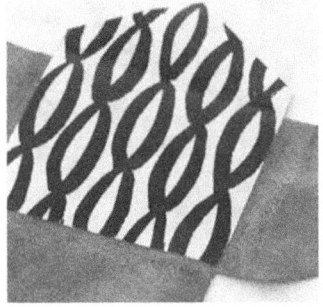

6. Next, puncture a hole at the end corners of your clutch with a leather hole punch. Now, you need to align the holes by folding the corners into the middle.

7. After that, place the screw back on the backside of the right corner on your clutch. Next, place the left corner on the top of your screw back. After, place the bottom corner on top, and finally, place the top corner on top of your screw back.

    Note: You should follow this particular order to get the correct shape of your leather clutch bag.

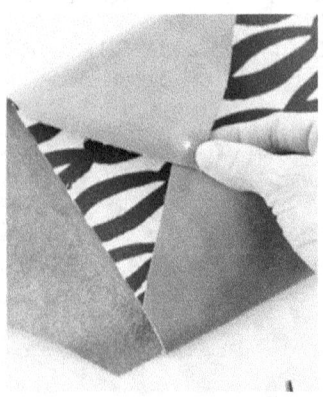

8. You are almost done. All you need to do is to screw the top of the screw back on its top to hold the corners of the clutch firmly at that point. Once it is firmly screwed in, your leather clutch bag is ready for use!

9. The picture below is the outcome of how your leather clutch bag should look like once you are done with the project.

Leather Mason Jar Sleeve

This leather project is super easy and does not require many tools. It is also scarce leatherwork and will make a perfect gift!

Supplies

- A leather punch
- X-acto knife
- A metal ruler
- A snaptool or setter tool
- A hammer
- Heavy-duty leather about one-eight inches thick
- Waxed cord
- Snap fasteners

Procedures

1. First things first, you need to do a bit of measuring and figuring. Cut out two rectangular-shaped pieces of leather. The first rectangular-shaped leather is for the sleeve of your project. To get the exact length of the sleeve leather, simply wrap it around the mason jar you want to make the leather sleeve and mark the size with a marker or sharpie. You can also decide to use the X-acto knife to make the mark on the leather. Depending on which one you prefer.
2. Next, measure the height you will need for the mason jar and mark the second rectangular leather.

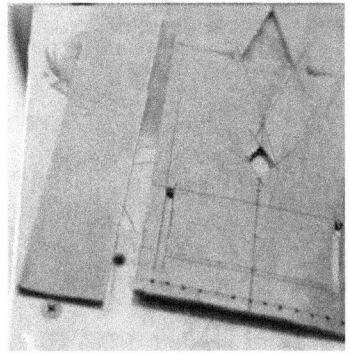

3. Next, scratch out your design, handle holes, and cut them out on the second rectangular-shaped leather you cut out. (You could use any method of your choosing, however, use something that doesn't stick out when you wrap it. A diagonal-shaped layout can be used because both ends are joint, so when wrapped around the mason jar, it won't stick out).

4. Next, cut out a piece that would work for your handle. You can decide to make a mock-up with paper. This will help you in figuring out the right proportions and measurements. Although not all mason jars are the same size, here are the measurements I used for my mason jar. The

sleeve measurement—(11 ⅛" x 3 ⅜"). The handle measurement—(11/4" x 10 ¼").

5. Next, puncture holes on both ends of the sleeve piece for the twine. After, you need to attach the snap to the handle. To do that, punch holes on one of the two ends on your handle piece. Those are the holes where you attach the snaps. You can decide to add a second snap for preferable aesthetics.

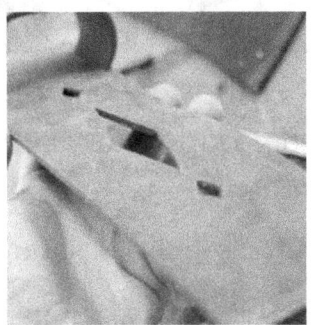

6. There are four pieces of snap you get when you purchase a set (stud, button, socket, and eyelet).

So what do you do next with the snaps? Place the 'button' snap on one side of the leather and place the socket snap on the other end. Ensure that the button side is where you want it. Place your setter on the socket snap, and using your hammer, give it a good smack. Redo this process with your other set (eyelet and stud) on the other end. Next, thread your handle through the sleeve and snap method.

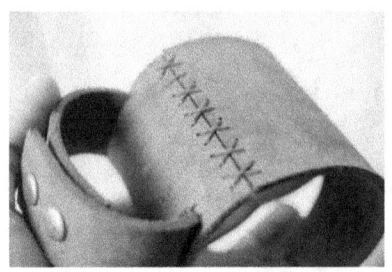

7. All you need to do is to place the two ends of your sleeve together. From the waxed cord, cut a couple of feet. Your lines should be stiff enough that you shouldn't need any needles. Start knotting the end from the inside using an 'X' pattern. The 'X' pattern is one of the most used in leather making for this type of project. Ensure that your laces are firmly in place.
8. You are done! Put your mason jar inside your leather mason jar sleeve.

Leather Magazine Holder

Supplies

- Four 16inches wooden dowel rods
- 2 wooden boards 8" by 18"
- Wood glue
- Medium sandpaper
- Wood stain
- Small bowl of 5.5 width
- Faux leather 13.5" by 42"
- Fabric glue
- Jigsaw
- 5/8" paddle bits
- Leather needles

- Sewing machine

Procedures

1. Cut your dowel rods and wooden plaques into the sizes you want to work with.
2. Use a small-sized bowl to trace half of the bowl's bottom outline on the surface of the wood.

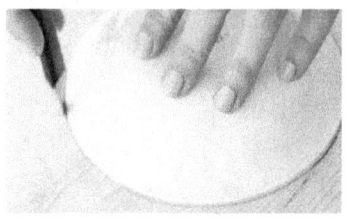

3. Now, trace the rest of the bowl and bottom outline above the half-circle you drew above.

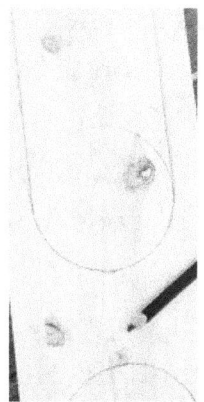

4. Draw out a straight line from either side of the circle and then extend it to the top of the wooden plaque.
5. Cut out the shapes from the wooden piece with a Jigsaw. Just ensure that while cutting, you follow the pencil marks and that the wooden plaque is fastened firmly to a surface so that it doesn't up shake as you run the blade of the saw through it.
6. When you are done with the procedure above, trace out the outline of the piece you just cut out on another wooden plaque with the aid of a pencil with a sharpened tip.
7. Now, cut out the outline you made with a jigsaw. You can follow the procedures above to help you with this.

8. To bore holes for the dowel rods, use a pencil to mark out points on the wooden plaque with each hole about 1.5" measured from the top and bottom of the wooden plaque. Then, then place a piece of scrap wood underneath the board, and the and then, the use a 5/8" paddle bit to bore holes through those marks. To do this, just drill the holes until the mouth of the bit passes through to the other side. Then, you can turn your board over, finish the drilling process from that side.

9. After drilling out the holes, use a sanding tool to smoothen the rough edges.
10. Then, stain the pieces evenly with a lint-free cloth. Add another layer of lacquer only after the first one dries.

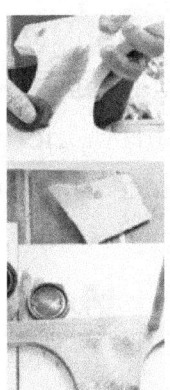

11. While you wait for the stain to dry, use a rotary cutter to cut your leather into the appropriate shape sizes.
12. Now, make a template on a sheet of paper with a dimension of 6" by 8". Then, you can place the template about two inches from either side of the sheet.

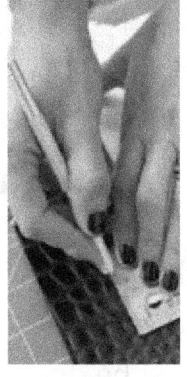

13. Cut around the template with an X-acto knife while it is secured in place with a tape aid.
14. Line up drops of fabric glue on the leather's insides at a distance of 1" from each of the outer edges. Fold the sides towards the inside while ensuring that the cut-outs are lined up together. This glue works to hold the leather as you sew through it.
15. Fix a leather needle to your sewing machine, but then use it to sew the pocket sides 1/2 inches from the folded piece's inner parts. These pockets you sew will help bear your dowel rods as you suspend the leather from the wooden frames.

16. After passing the rods through the pockets, gather up the magazine holder by fixing the dowels into the holes at each of the corners. This procedure must be done while the dowels are still

bearing the leather strips. Then, additional bits of glue to the hole to finish attaching the dowels.
17. Leave the glue to dry and then, wipe off the excess adhesive with a dry towel.
18. You are done.

Mini Leather Pouch

Supplies

- Scrap leather
- Pencil
- Ruler
- Knife
- Scissors
- Paper punch

Procedures

1. Cut out four small leather strips—two should be the same size (for the body), one should be for the closure part and one more for the flap.

2. Arrange the strips for the body in the same line, with the wrong sides facing each other.
3. Place the leather strip that you want to use for closure on the top piece.

4. Place the strips of leather on a cutting board and use a paper punch to make holes along the sides you want to stitch through.

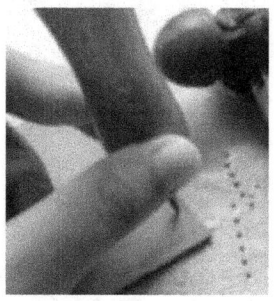

5. Set your needle and thread before going ahead to make blanket stitches along the sides of the body that will hold the closure strips together.
6. Tie a knot at the end of the thread before cutting off the excess thread.
7. Fix the strip of leather for the flap at the central portion of the strip. To fix the flap to the pouch, make cross stitches.

8. You are done!

Yoga Mat Strap

Supplies

- Two pieces of leather—29" by 1"
- One piece of leather—19" by 1"
- Permanent marker
- Leather Punch
- Extra strong thread

Procedures

1. This project will help you carry your mat easily to your next yoga class. You will start by marking points ¼", 1", five ¼" and 6" from one end of the 29" by 1" leather strip.
2. Use the leather punch tool to make holes in the four points you marked out. Repeat this procedure on both pieces of leather.
3. Fold the leather in such a way that the holes punched into it are aligned. Then, use thick strings of thread to sew one end of the

leatherback and forth. This technique will help the leather to be secured.
4. Take the opposite ends of the leather strip, and then pass them through the loops you created by stitching the folds together.
5. Now, on both ends of the 19" piece and the open ends of the 29" work, mark out four dots arranged in squares.
6. Use a leather punch to punch holes through the marks you created.
7. Lastly, use the thread strings to sew a secure 'X' through the punched-out holes.
8. You are done.

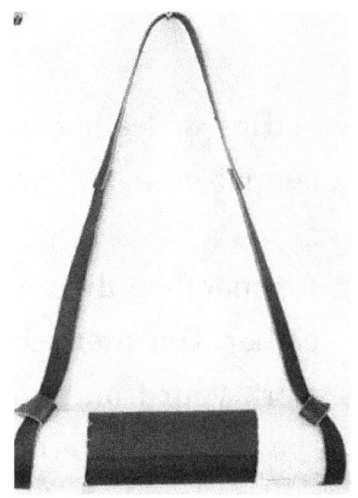

Fold-Over Clutch

Supplies

- Hot pink faux leather (half a yard)
- Stiff iron
- A zipper of about 16 inches in length
- Sewing machine
- Cutting board
- Needle and thread
- Pins

Procedures

1. Cut out two strips of leather and two strips of interfacing material, each of a dimension of 12" by 13."
2. Use an iron to smoothen the wrong side of each piece of the leather. The interface side should face you as you work your iron on it. It should also adhere to the back of the material.

3. Lay the zipper to the right with its side up, and then go ahead to align one piece of the leather with the interfacing material so that their bottoms lie on the same line. They then run pins along the bottom edge.
4. Sew the pinned ends with your zipper foot running across those lines.
5. Take the second leather strip and the interfacing material, and then repeat the procedure above. While you do this, ensure that the right side of the leather is well aligned with the right side of the zipper. Then, use your zipper foot to sew across that edge.
6. Once the zipper is at the very top, pin the three ends. Then, push the zipper halfway up and sew along those three ends.
7. Trim the edges of your project before turning it so that the inside is not outside. You can then go-ahead to tuck in the edges so that it comes out more sharply.
8. You are done!

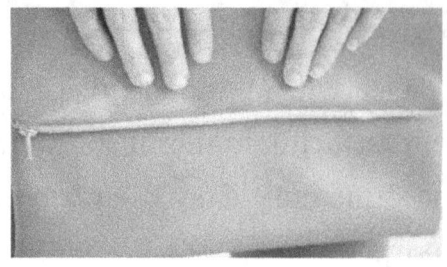

Mouse Pad

Supplies

- Leather
- Cork
- Spray adhesive

Procedures

1. Trace out the outline of your mousepad with a small box with a rectangular base. This outline will be your template.

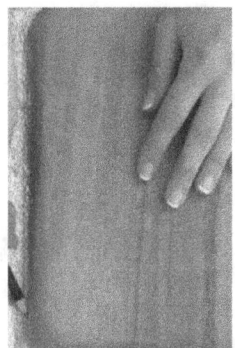

2. Cut out the outline of the template while following the lines you marked out.
3. Spray a piece of cork with an aerosol adhesive. Aerosol adhesives aren't as thick as the regular glue, so it ends up penetrating the leather strips more deeply and thoroughly. It will also not seep through the cork's holes.

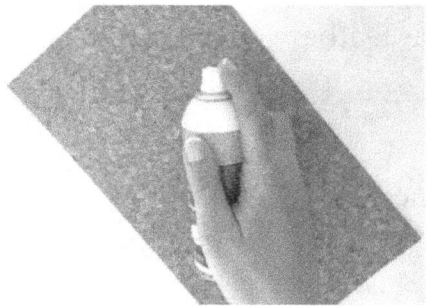

4. Now, press the leather onto the surface of the cork with the glue. Then, trim off the cork's excesses.

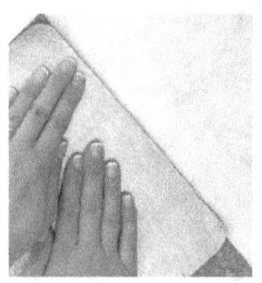
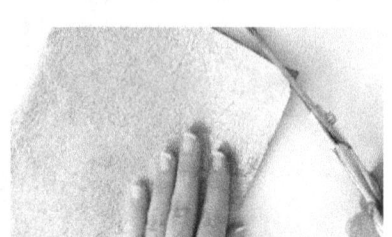

5. You are done.

Leather Studded Bracelet

Supplies

- A thin leather strip.
- Hammer
- Pins
- Magnetic closures.
- Leather studs
- Pliers.
- Leather hole punch
- Leather glue
- Pen

Procedures

1. Mark out the locations for the studs on your leather strip with the aid of a pen.

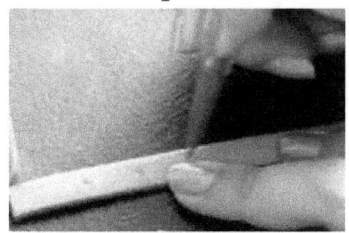

2. Punch out holes through those points with a leather hole punch.

3. Fix the leather studs through each of the holes.

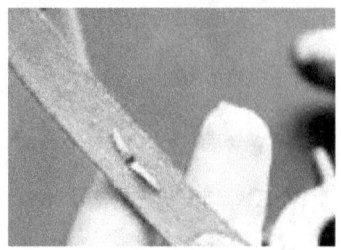

4. Apply the right quantity of glue to the ends of the leather strip, and then push the clasps.

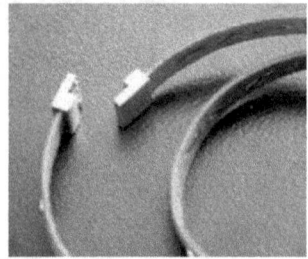

5. Let the glue dry totally.
6. You are done!

Chapter 6

Fixing Common Leathercraft Problems

1. Using blunt tools for your projects can make it very difficult for you to get good results. So, to get something that catches the eye of people, you have to ensure that you know how to sharpen your cutting tools. Also, going for cheap tools may not be the best option for you. Since you will just be getting them once, why not just go for the best? Most of the cheap tools come out with dull blades from their boxes and are usually of low quality. The more you spend on your tools at the purchase point, the more quality your projects will be.
2. Inconsistency: You should ensure that you carry out your operations the same way throughout

your projects. This issue is very common in hand stitching where one will see several stitch lines running across the surface of your projects.
3. In a situation where you make a mistake while stamping a design to your project, you can follow the guidelines below to fix it.

- Moisten the spot again, and then, use the flat edge of a slick tool or a bone folder to scrub at the mistake until most of it has vanished.
- Then, you can go ahead to stamp the leather again.

4. To get rid of tool marks from the surface of your leather strip, you can follow the guidelines below:

- Dampen the area with sprays of water. This technique will help the area with the mark to swell up considerably.
- To prevent water stains from ruining the outlook of your leather projects, ensure that you wet the whole project.
- Use a bone folder to rub across the surface of the leather while it is saturated with moisture.
- Leave the leather to dry. You could stretch out the edges and then, have them pinned down so

that the moisture in it can evaporate pretty quickly.

The end... almost!

Hey! We've made it to the final chapter of this book, and I hope you've enjoyed it so far.

If you have not done so yet, I would be incredibly thankful if you could take just a minute to leave a quick review on Amazon

Reviews are not easy to come by, and as an independent author with a little marketing budget, I rely on you, my readers, to leave a short review on Amazon.

Even if it is just a sentence or two!

So if you really enjoyed this book, please...

\>\> Click here to leave a brief review on Amazon.

I truly appreciate your effort to leave your review, as it truly makes a huge difference.

Chapter 7

Leathercraft Frequently Asked Questions

1. **What are the basic tools needed for leather crafting?**

   As a beginner, you will need the following tools: awls, bevellers, burnishing tools, cutters, gouges, glues, groovers, mauls, pricking irons, punches, skivers, stamps, sewing accessories, and cutting mats. The awls are necessary to make the holes you make on your leather strip with a paper punch wider. Burnishing tools will help to melt the edges of your leather to prevent them from melting.

2. **What things can be made with the leatherworking principle?**

   This craft is one general-purpose craft that can be used to make items like coats, cloaks, leather bags, leather purses, armors, vehicle upholstery, armor kits, and so on.

3. **How can I finish the edges of my leather project?**

   The best technique that you can use to finish the edges of leather is known as the burnishing technique. Here, we will run through a guide that will help you with the process of burnishing.

   - Cut out the needed strips of leather neatly and in measured dimensions. To make clean cuts, ensure that you sharpen the edges of your tools regularly. Then, ensure that you make templates of the design you want etched out on your leather. Keep score of your cuts by using a metal-edged ruler alongside the razor blades you use for cutting. If you are using knives to cut, run the tips through the outlines softly before proceeding to making deeper cuts. This technique will help solve the issue where your knife slips from the grooves. You could also make your cutting job very easy by dampening the leather strips before you cut through them.
   - To prevent the edges of your project from splitting apart during the process of burnishing them, ensure that you glue the joints to the very

end. Glue the edges in bits to prevent the glue from spreading over to the rest of the project. For this technique, you can use cement glue.
- Check the edges of your project to see that everything is well aligned. Any error can be corrected by sanding the edges though. You could also use your knife to cut out any edge that pops out from the regular line, to get flat surfaces.
- Now, the next thing to do is to bevel the edges of your projects. Beveling just involves the rounding of the edges of your project. If you don't do this technique before you burnish your leather, the edges will end up folding over on themselves.
- Sand the edges of your project until they are well-leveled. Sanding also helps to get rid of the excess glue from the edges of your project! The glue usually comes out as obvious because it shows up as dark spots on the leather strip.
- Dye your projects with wool daubers.
- Then, burnish your tool with the aid of a wood slicker. The details of this procedure have already been discussed in this book, so, you can just read through it and use it as a guide.

- Lastly, apply beeswax to the surface of your project to finish it. Then, you can buff out the excesses with a strip of lint-free cloth.

4. **Do the edges of leather strips fray when you cut through them?**

   If you are working with smooth leather, you can be sure that it won't fray. The only ones that fray is the artificial ones like suede.

5. **Is beeswax compatible with leather?**

   Yes, it is. It is used as a finish that helps your project to repel water and to keep the leather strip soft and supple. To apply beeswax to the surface of your project, use a soft and clean cloth that has been previously dipped inside the beeswax. Roll it in circles about the surface, and then, buss off the excesses with a lint-free cloth. This way, the grains, texture, and color of your leather strip remain soft and well-conditioned.

6. **What tool can be used to cut through leather?**
   The best knives for this purpose are utility knives and craft knives. The other ones you could work

with include rotary cutters, and heavy-duty scissors.

Conclusion

Throughout this book, we have been able to establish the fact that leather crafting is a process of cutting through leather to make fabulous designs. Mind you, the art doesn't just involve you making cuttings. You could do other things like stamping, dyeing, gluing, burnishing, stitching, coloring, and finishing of leather. The art of crafting with leather can be the most interesting thing to do, but then, you will need to ensure that you take utmost care in learning every detail and technique. Most of the tips listed here will help you avoid most of the preliminary errors, but then, it is expected that after a few consistent efforts of practicing, you should be able to add more to the list.

Also, in case you try out any project here, and eventually, come out with a result that does only little to fascinate you, go on and do it again. Practice they say makes perfect. After exhausting all the projects in this book, you can go on and further engage your sense of creativity. Make several templates of designs, and make them with leather.

Happy Crafting!

www.ingramcontent.com/pod-product-compliance
Lightning Source LLC
Chambersburg PA
CBHW062033120526
44592CB00036B/2032